I0426407

Estimating Bird Density and Detection Probability at Five National Park Units in Southern Oregon and Northern California

Natural Resource Technical Report NPS/KLMN/NRTR—2013/699

Jaime L. Stephens[1], Sean R. Mohren[2], Daniel C. Barton[1], John D. Alexander[1], and Daniel A. Sarr[2]

Klamath Bird Observatory[1]
PO Box 758
Ashland, OR 97520

Klamath Inventory and Monitoring Network, NPS[2]
1250 Siskiyou Blvd
Ashland, OR 97520

February 2013

U.S. Department of the Interior
National Park Service
Natural Resource Stewardship and Science
Fort Collins, Colorado

The National Park Service, Natural Resource Stewardship and Science office in Fort Collins, Colorado, publishes a range of reports that address natural resource topics. These reports are of interest and applicability to a broad audience in the National Park Service and others in natural resource management, including scientists, conservation and environmental constituencies, and the public.

The Natural Resource Technical Report Series is used to disseminate results of scientific studies in the physical, biological, and social sciences for both the advancement of science and the achievement of the National Park Service mission. The series provides contributors with a forum for displaying comprehensive data that are often deleted from journals because of page limitations.

All manuscripts in the series receive the appropriate level of peer review to ensure that the information is scientifically credible, technically accurate, appropriately written for the intended audience, and designed and published in a professional manner. Data in this report were collected and analyzed using methods based on established, peer-reviewed protocols and were analyzed and interpreted within the guidelines of the protocols. This report received formal peer review by subject-matter experts who were not directly involved in the collection, analysis, or reporting of the data, and whose background and expertise put them on par technically and scientifically with the authors of the information.

Views, statements, findings, conclusions, recommendations, and data in this report do not necessarily reflect views and policies of the National Park Service, U.S. Department of the Interior. Mention of trade names or commercial products does not constitute endorsement or recommendation for use by the U.S. Government.

This report is available from the Klamath Network website (http://science.nature.nps.gov/im/units/klmn/monitoring/vs/landbird/vs_landbirds.cfm) and the Natural Resource Publications Management website (http://www.nature.nps.gov/publications/nrpm/).

Please cite this publication as:

Stephens, J. L., S. R. Mohren, D. C. Barton, J. D. Alexander, and D. A. Sarr. 2013. Estimating bird density and detection probability at five national park units in southern Oregon and northern California. Natural Resource Technical Report NPS/KLMN/NRTR—2013/699. National Park Service, Fort Collins, Colorado.

February 2013

Contents

	Page
Figures	iv
Tables	iv
Abstract	v
Acknowledgments	vi
Introduction	1
Methods	3
Study Sites and Sampling Design	3
Bird Surveys	3
Data Analysis	3
Results	7
Discussion	17
Literature Cited	18

Figures

Page

Figure 1. Observed (bars) and expected (curves) distributions of observations by distance 13

Figure 2. Relationship between log density estimates from models of all detections and log density estimates from song detections (multiplied by 2 to account for non-singing females) 15

Figure 3. Proportion of song detections in each sample (Freeman-Tukey double-arcsine transformed) and the difference between log density of total detections and log density of song detections are negatively correlated (N = 25, r = -0.53, p = 0.006; Figure 2)... 16

Tables

Page

Table 1. Detectability models, density estimates, confidence intervals, effective detection radius (EDR), and goodness of fit statistics for all detections by species and park 8

Table 1 (continued). Detectability models, density estimates, confidence intervals, effective detection radius (EDR), and goodness of fit statistics for all detections by species and park 9

Table 2. Detectability models, density estimates, confidence intervals, effective detection radius (EDR), and goodness of fit statistics for song detections by species and park... 10

Abstract

As part of the national Inventory and Monitoring Program of the National Park Service, the Klamath Inventory and Monitoring Network and Klamath Bird Observatory established a protocol to monitor long-term status and trends in landbird populations at National Park units in southern Oregon and northern California. This report examines detection probabilities and estimates densities using data from the first sequence of surveys in the five larger park units in the Network: Crater Lake National Park, Lassen Volcanic National Park, Lava Beds National Monument, Redwood National and State Parks, and Whiskeytown National Recreation Area. At each park, 25–35 sites were established using a stratified random approach. Breeding season point counts were conducted at each park from 2008–2010, along with the collection of vegetation data. For this analysis we examined factors related to detection probability using distance sampling. A number of factors were related to detection probability, including observer and type of detection. Effective distance radii varied among species suggesting that counts may not be proportionate based on a fixed radius. On the other hand, detection models fit the data poorly for some species, which showed evidence of observer avoidance or heaping, especially for song detections. Density estimates for all detections were highly correlated with song-based density estimates, and differences between the two estimates were related to the proportion of song detections. Model assumptions for distance sampling may not always be met, and our results suggest density estimates from this single year of surveys should be interpreted with caution. In the future, approaches of combining detections across years or park units may provide more robust estimates. Indices such as relative abundance remain useful in some contexts, and comparisons are needed with independently derived measures of density from spot-mapping. These results highlight the importance of considering differences among species in detection type and detection distances, as well as designing sampling to minimize observer effects.

Acknowledgments

We would like to acknowledge Felicity Newell for her assistance with this report. Implementation of the monitoring program would not have been possible without the help of the park staff. Special thanks for logistical support in 2008: J. Roth, K. Schmidt, A. Transou, S. Mark, S. Powell, T. Hines, J. Wartella, S. Mclaughlin, J. McClelland, B. Silver, G. Holm, D. Hays, and D. Larson; in 2009: B. Alberti, J. Gibson, J. Richardson, J. Roth, and R. Weatherbee; and in 2010: D. Clayton, G. Holm, M. Magnuson, J. Roth, and L. Vella. Additional thanks to Cave Research Foundation at Lava Beds National Monument for use of the Cave Research Center and accommodations. The dedication of the field crews made this research successful. Point count surveys in 2008 were completed by L. Hammer, J. Kellerman, and F. Lospalluto; in 2009 by L. Hammer and J. DeStaebler, and in 2010 by J. DeStaebler, G. Gardner, I. Koski, and F. Lospalluto. This report was improved with the help of comments from T. Rodhouse.

Introduction

Preserving natural resources unimpaired for the enjoyment, education and inspiration of this and future generations is part of the mission of the National Park Service (NPS). In an effort to ensure that this mission is met, the NPS developed the Inventory and Monitoring (I&M) Program in which parks are organized into 32 networks for environmental inventory and monitoring. In 2002, the Klamath Inventory and Monitoring Network (KLMN), working with park resources staff and outside experts identified a suite of vital signs that could be examined in concert with each other to provide accurate, ecologically meaningful, and defensible estimates of park ecosystem integrity (Odion et al. 2005, Sarr et al. 2007). As part of this selection process, bird communities were ranked number four in importance because populations and compositions of bird communities can be easily monitored and can be related to changing environmental conditions. Beginning in 2008, the KLMN and Klamath Bird Observatory (KBO) developed a long-term monitoring protocol to examine status and trends of landbird populations at six National Park units in southern Oregon and northern California (Stephens et al. 2010a, b). The landbird monitoring program was designed to contribute to the vital signs monitoring program of the KLMN (Sarr et al. 2007), and meet objectives for both the NPS as a whole (Fancy and Sauer 2000), as well as regional and national bird monitoring goals identified by Partners in Flight (PIF) (Altman 1999, 2000, CalPIF 2002a, b, 2004, Rich et al. 2004, Hussell and Ralph 2005, CalPIF 2005, Sarr et al. 2011).

Five park units are included in this report. Two National Parks, Crater Lake National Park (CRLA) and Lassen Volcanic National Park (LAVO), are characterized by high elevation coniferous forests of the Cascade Range with elevations up to 3,200 m. Lava Beds National Monument (LABE), located at slightly lower elevation on the dry Modoc Plateau, is dominated by open shrub-steppe sagebrush. Redwood National and State Parks (RNSP) is near sea level and supports areas of old-growth coastal redwoods. Whiskeytown National Recreation Area (WHIS) includes mixed conifer forest, oak woodland and chaparral centered on Whiskeytown Lake.

Estimating bird densities as a measure of ecosystem health and function was identified as a key component of bird monitoring by the KLMN. However, detectability is an important issue in population monitoring (Buckland et al. 2001, Buckland et al. 2004); often birds targeted for surveys may be present but undetected, and this can bias the results of surveys. Variation in detection probability among survey locations, if unaccounted for, may further complicate the ability to interpret findings (but not always; see Johnson 2008). This variation in detectability may confound the monitoring questions of interest, which can result in false acceptance or rejection of hypotheses about trends in abundance or variation among sampling units (Thompson and LaSorte 2008). A wide variety of approaches have been applied to this problem in wildlife and conservation biology (Mills 2012), including mark-recapture methodologies, intensive census techniques (e.g. spot-mapping) that ensure detectability is at or near 1 (e.g. DeSante 1986), and survey techniques that allow for the estimation of detectability (Rosenstock et al. 2002). In this report, we examined detectability of bird species at each of the 5 park units (CRLA, LABE, ORCA, RNSP, WHIS) and estimated bird densities to inform future analysis and synthesis reports. Specifically, to examine detection probability, we used variable circular plot (VCP) data to model detection functions and using those functions, we evaluated alternative approaches to estimating bird densities based on distance sampling (Buckland et al. 2001, Buckland et al. 2004).

Methods

Study Sites and Sampling Design

We used standard bird monitoring techniques to sample breeding birds within the park units. A brief description of the site selection process and sampling design is provided below and a detailed description can be found in the KLMN Landbird Monitoring Protocol (Stephens et al. 2010a) and the Establishment of Survey Sites for Monitoring Landbirds within the Klamath Network (Stephens et al. 2010b).

At each of the five larger parks included in this analysis, 25 – 35 sites were established using a balanced sampling design approach (Stephens et al. 2010b). Generally, at each site, 12 point count stations were established within close proximity using a systematic approach, in some instances logistical constraints limited sampling to only 4–9 points at a site (Stephens et al. 2010b). Stations were arranged 250 m apart from one another to minimize the likelihood of double counting birds (Scott et al. 1981).

Bird Surveys

From 2008-2010, a single survey was conducted at a total of 1,618 point count stations at 149 sites during the first sequence of visits to each KLMN park. Two park units were surveyed in 2008 (RNSP and LABE), one in 2009 (WHIS), and two in 2010 (CRLA and LAVO). Point count stations were sampled during the breeding season (early May through July) following the variable circular plot methodology that incorporates distance sampling (Reynolds et al. 1980, Fancy 1997, Nelson and Fancy 1999). Each park was surveyed by two experienced observers trained on bird identification and distance estimation. Counts were conducted within the first 4 hours after sunrise, and surveys were not conducted during inclement weather. All birds seen or heard during a 5-minute count period were identified to species. Distance to the nearest meter and type of detection (e.g. song, call, visual) were recorded, as well as any evidence of breeding (e.g., carrying nest material, copulation) (Stephens et al. 2010a).

Data Analysis

We estimated densities of bird species within sampling frames at each park using distance sampling (Reynolds et al. 1980, Buckland et al. 2001, Stephens et al. 2010a). Generally, distance sampling assumes that detection probability of a bird present and available for detection is 1 near the observer and declines monotonically as a function of increasing distance. Estimating the probability of detection using distance sampling allows for the estimation of true density, by estimating the total number of individuals present and available for detection within the area effectively surveyed. While it is common and often informative to assume that simple count data is proportional to true density and that detectability <1 is similar or equivalent among units of analysis (sites) over time (years) (i.e. studies of relative abundance; Johnson 2008), this assumption is often violated in empirical studies (Norvell et al. 2003) and thus estimates of density are confounded with variation in detectability and cannot be reliably used to infer variation in density over space and time. Density estimation using distance sampling provides an alternative to studies of relative abundance, because density estimation allows for variation in detectability across units of analysis, and thus allows for non-proportionality between simple counts and true density (Buckland et al. 2001, Buckland et al. 2004.

We tested the *a priori* hypotheses that detection probability will vary by species, observer, sampling frame, and detection type (i.e., song, call, or visual) because of differences in how individual species vocalizations carry, habitat, and observer skill or hearing ability (Stephens et al. 2010a). We used multiple covariate distance sampling (MCDS) in Program Distance (Thomas et al. 2010) to fit detection functions to the observed data separately for each species and to test the importance of environmental and observer factors thought to influence detection probability. Inspection of the distribution of observed data by species, observer, sampling frame, and detection type was used to identify potential violations of some of the assumptions of distance sampling (caused by avoidance behavior or 'heaping' of observations on preferred distance values such that there is an unnatural number of detections at a given distance, often at 50 m; see Buckland et al. 2001). When violations of assumptions occur, model fit can be improved by combining continuous data into intervals, an approach we used when data distributions suggested avoidance or heaping. Model fit is also frequently improved by removing a proportion of the most distant detections (commonly 10%), and, when appropriate, we applied this approach following Buckland et al. (2001). We then fit models using maximum likelihood and compared the relative support of alternative models using Akaike's Information Criterion (AIC; Burnham and Anderson 2002). We assessed goodness of fit using Chi-square and Cramer-von Mises family tests (Buckland et al. 2001). The Cramer-von Mises family tests are not applicable to data pooled into intervals, and thus we only used this method when assessing models of continuous data.

We fit alternative models to the observed distribution of detections using half-normal or hazard key functions with cosine or Hermite polynomial adjustment terms, which contained factorial effects of observer, sampling frame, and/or detection type on the scale parameter of the model (Buckland et al. 2004). We allowed a maximum of two adjustment parameters in each model, but constrained the number of adjustment parameters to 0 when adjustment parameters resulted in fitting models that were not monotonically decreasing (an assumption of distance analysis; Marques et al. 2007). We also compared support for models that estimated detectability separately for different sampling frames (stratification), because specifying sampling frames as a factor in MCDS only allows for effects of sampling frame on the scale parameter of the detection function. When the distributions of detection distances were highly heterogeneous among sampling frames within a single species, we conducted analyses separately for each frame to allow alternative interval assignments and truncation to improve model fit. In some cases we also analyzed data separately to improve convergence of a model on the maximum-likelihood parameter estimates. We report analytical density estimates, analytical 95% confidence intervals, and effective detection radius (EDR) for each species from the model(s) that were best supported by AIC that also showed reasonable goodness of fit (P > 0.20). Reported densities are the product of density of detections and the mean number of individuals in each detection when the numbers of paired or flock detections was small (in species that do not commonly flock), and are corrected for group-size bias in detectability when the numbers of flocks was large (such as in flocking finch species; Buckland et al. 2001). We further report parameter estimates from poor-fitting models when no model fit the data well, but we suggest these results be interpreted with caution. Non-independence of points within sites was explicitly accounted for in this analysis by estimating the variance of the encounter rate from the sample variance in encounter rate between sites, and bootstrap variances were calculated by resampling entire sites (rather than individual points) with replacement (Thomas et al. 2010). This approach inflates the estimated variance and confidence intervals of density, reflecting the non-independence of data included in the analysis. The analyses were constrained to species which had > 80 total detections in at least one sampling frame because of difficulties with estimating detectability and density with small numbers of detections.

We also used a bootstrapping approach implemented in Program Distance to estimate density via an alternative approach that is robust to violation of the assumption that the true sampling variance is equal to the theoretical sampling variance (overdispersion). We used 1000 bootstrap replicates to estimate densities and confidence intervals following Buckland et al. (2001) and Thomas et al. (2010). We report these bootstrap densities and confidence intervals alongside analytical densities and confidence intervals. Bootstrap subsamples for some species did not converge on maximum-likelihood parameter estimates, which resulted in our inability to apply this technique to all species.

Alternative detection cues (singing, calling, or visual) may have very different detection probabilities (Marques et al. 2007). Since only males of most temperate territorial bird species sing, females are unavailable for detection via singing, yet singing is likely the most easily detected cue. Yet, all individuals in the population are available for detection via calling or visual cues but detection probability of these cues may vary with sex (i.e. females may visually be cryptic or may have different calling rates than males). This interaction between detection probability of the sexes and detection type has led researchers to either use all detections to estimate total density, or to use singing detections only, sometimes on the basis of rules regarding the proportion of detections of different types (e.g. DeSante 1986). Some researchers who took the latter approach then doubled the estimated density of singing males as an estimator of total density, which implicitly assumes that all singing males represent pairs (e.g. Emlen 1971). To compare these two techniques for estimating density and to avoid potentially arbitrary decisions about how to best estimate density, we conducted our model-fitting process for all detection cues (singing, calling, visual), and then repeated the process for singing birds alone. We conducted this analysis only in species that have identifiable territorial songs and for which there were sufficient numbers of observations with different detection cues. We then estimated the strength of the correlation between the two density estimates – one from all detections, one from songs only – across different species and sampling frames. We also tested whether the proportion of song detections was correlated with the size of the discrepancy between the two density estimates, to examine whether rules applied in studies such as DeSante (1986) are appropriate for use in estimating density in Klamath Network parks. This analysis should help inform the most appropriate technique for estimating density in future products of the Landbird Monitoring Protocol of the KLMN (Stephens et al. 2010a).

Results

Analytical and bootstrap density estimates, 95% confidence intervals, EDR, goodness of fit statistics, and model specifications are reported from the best models using all detections for 31 species in five parks in Table 1. This represented 8–23% of the species detected on point counts at each park; with additional data in future years more species may be analyzed. The same parameters from the best models considered for detectability and density using song detections for 19 species are reported in Table 2. We did not model song-only densities for 12 species which included those without an identifiable territorial song or where both sexes sing, and excluding non-song detections resulted in an inability to estimate a detectability function due to small sample size or poor fit.

Estimated densities using all detections varied widely among species (0.05 – 14.7 birds / ha; Table 1) and among parks within species (e.g. Oregon Junco and Pine Siskin; Table 1). Effective detection radius (EDR) also varied widely among species and among parks within species (Table 1). The same wide variation existed in density estimates and EDR estimated from song detections (Table 2). Effects of observer on the scaling parameter of the detectability function were frequently included in the best model, suggesting that observer has strong effects on estimates of detectability (Tables 1, 2).

Table 1. Detectability models, density estimates, confidence intervals, effective detection radius (EDR), and goodness of fit statistics for all detections by species and park. The best model selected through an information-theoretic and goodness of fit model selection process is shown. Model-fitting issues that may affect interpretability are shown in addition to goodness of fit statistics.

Common name	Park	Key / adj.[1]	Model[2]	K	Density (birds/ha)	95 % CI	Bootstrap density (birds/ha)	95 % CI	EDR (m)	X^2 GOF p	Cramer-von Mises GOF p	Model issues[3]
American Robin	CRLA	HZ C	S + O	6	0.45	(0.35 - 0.59)	0.53	(0.28 - 0.99)	49.40	0.14		
	LAVO				0.43	(0.35 - 0.52)	0.52	(0.32 - 0.86)	49.40	0.14		
Audubon's Warbler	CRLA	HZ C	F * (S + O)	8	1.35	(1.19 - 1.53)	1.39	(1.04 - 1.96)	43.33	0.22		C, I
	LAVO				0.44	(0.34 - 0.56)	0.43	(0.25 - 0.83)	69.94	0.00		
Black-headed Grosbeak	WHIS	HN C	S + O	3	0.28	(0.24 - 0.33)	0.30	(0.20 - 0.43)	80.35	0.40	0.60	
Black-throated Gray Warbler	WHIS	HN C	S + O	3	0.88	(0.75 - 1.02)	0.83	(0.43 - 1.21)	57.74	0.78		—
Brewer's Sparrow	LABE	HZ C	S	3	0.09	(0.08 - 0.11)	0.10	(0.02 - 0.21)	94.81	0.06	0.03	
Brown-headed Cowbird	LABE	HN C	O	2	0.16	(0.13 - 0.21)	0.20	(0.09 - 0.39)	61.28	0.56	0.80	
Cassin's Vireo	WHIS	HN C	S	2	0.24	(0.20 - 0.29)	0.26	(0.15 - 0.43)	67.81	0.15	0.70	
Chestnut-backed Chickadee	RNSP	HN C	O	2	0.75	(0.63 - 0.90)	0.89	(0.46 - 1.64)	49.44	0.23	0.50	
Golden-crowned Kinglet	CRLA	HN C	O	2	3.37	(2.47 - 4.59)	3.38	(2.09 - 4.81)	13.80	0.54		
	LAVO	HN C	-	1	0.46	(0.35 - 0.62)	0.38	(0.06 - 0.67)	43.26	0.61		—
Gray Jay	CRLA	HN C	O	2	0.44	(0.36 - 0.55)	0.44	(0.31 - 0.59)	45.10	0.22	0.15	C
Hermit Thrush	CRLA	HN C	S + O	3	0.38	(0.33 - 0.44)			71.54	0.01		C, B, I
Lazuli Bunting	LABE	HN C	S + O	3	0.58	(0.44 - 0.77)			51.91	0.03		C, B, I
Lesser Goldfinch	WHIS	HZ C	-	2	0.29	(0.21 - 0.41)	0.30	(0.14 - 0.50)	53.21	0.52	0.90	
Lincoln's Sparrow	LAVO	HN C	S + O	3	0.80	(0.60 - 1.08)	0.83	(0.43 - 1.33)	46.02	0.29	0.40	

[1] Key / adjustment functions of models are abbreviated as: HN C = half-normal cosine, HZ C = hazard cosine.

[2] Model scale parameter covariates and stratification terms, abbreviated as: F = frame, S = song / non-song detection, C = call / not-call detection, O = observer. F * O indicates, for example, that the best model was stratified by frame and contained an effect of observer on the scale parameter that varied by frame. A '-' indicates no covariates were included in the best model.

[3] Model issues are abbreviated as follows: C = model constrained to have no adjustment parameters, B = bootstrap density estimates did not converge on maximum likelihood values, I = data pooled into intervals because of evidence of avoidance or heaping.

8

Table 1 (continued). Detectability models, density estimates, confidence intervals, effective detection radius (EDR), and goodness of fit statistics for all detections by species and park. The best model selected through an information-theoretic and goodness of fit model selection process is shown. Model-fitting issues that may affect interpretability are shown in addition to goodness of fit statistics.

Common name	Park	Key / adj.[1]	Model[2]	K	Density (birds/ha)	95 % CI	Bootstrap density (birds/ha)	95 % CI	EDR (m)	X^2 GOF p	Cramer-von Mises GOF p	Model issues[3]
Mountain Chickadee	CRLA	HZ C	O	3	3.02	(2.65 - 3.44)	3.25	(2.18 - 4.72)	26.31	0.42		
	LAVO	HZ C	O	4	0.33	(0.29 - 0.37)	0.28	(0.17 - 0.43)	78.49	0.27		
Orange-crowned Warbler	WHIS	HZ C	S + O	4	0.52	(0.41 - 0.64)	0.60	(0.32 - 1.16)	61.69	0.40	0.90	C
Oregon Junco	CRLA	HZ C	S + O	4	1.53	(1.30 - 1.80)	1.75	(1.11 - 2.66)	38.97	0.03	0.30	C
	LAVO	HZ C	S + O	4	1.88	(1.62 - 2.18)	1.94	(1.15 - 2.77)	38.76	0.00	0.15	C
	WHIS	HZ C	S	3	0.29	(0.22 - 0.38)	0.32	(0.12 - 0.83)	56.78	0.32	0.80	
Pacific Wren	RNSP	HZ C	S + O	4	0.62	(0.51 - 0.74)	0.74	(0.32 - 1.24)	66.03	0.03	0.50	C
Pacific-slope Flycatcher	RNSP	HZ C	-	2	1.51	(1.10 - 2.07)	1.53	(1.18 - 2.00)	50.05	0.04	0.90	
Pine Siskin	CRLA	HZ C	O	3	14.7	(13.0 - 16.5)	15.8	(12.3 - 20.6)	25.34	0.01		C, I
	LAVO	HZ C	-	2	0.39	(0.28 - 0.54)	0.41	(0.26 - 0.64)	59.41	0.10		
Spotted Towhee	LABE	HZ C	S + O	4	0.82	(0.76 - 0.88)	3.10	(0.35 - 1.31)	73.34	0.24		I
	WHIS	HZ C	S + O	4	0.41	(0.34 - 0.49)	0.39	(0.23 - 0.69)	67.25	0.01		
Steller's Jay	CRLA	HN C	F * O	8	0.24	(0.18 - 0.31)			55.51	0.00	0.10	C, B
	LAVO				0.17	(0.14 - 0.19)			91.80	0.02	0.20	
	RNSP				0.32	(0.27 - 0.38)			80.39	0.33	0.40	
	WHIS				0.09	(0.08 - 0.11)			92.76	0.06	0.90	
Swainson's Thrush	RNSP	HN C	S + O	3	0.16	(0.12 - 0.20)			99.72	0.77	0.40	B
Varied Thrush	RNSP	HZ C	S + O	4	0.18	(0.14 - 0.23)	0.19	(0.11 - 0.32)	95.93	0.20	0.90	C
Warbling Vireo	LAVO	HZ C	S	3	0.27	(0.20 - 0.38)	0.25	(0.13 - 0.45)	68.72	0.33	0.50	
Western Meadowlark	LABE	HZ C	S + O	4	0.27	(0.24 - 0.29)			152.90	0.06		B, I

[1] Key / adjustment functions of models are abbreviated as: HN C = half-normal cosine, HZ C = hazard cosine.

[2] Model scale parameter covariates and stratification terms, abbreviated as: F = frame, S = song / non-song detection, C = call / not-call detection, O = observer. F * O indicates, for example, that the best model was stratified by frame and contained an effect of observer on the scale parameter that varied by frame. A '-' indicates no covariates were included in the best model.

[3] Model issues are abbreviated as follows: C = model constrained to have no adjustment parameters, B = bootstrap density estimates did not converge on maximum likelihood values, I = data pooled into intervals because of evidence of avoidance or heaping.

9

Table 2. Detectability models, density estimates, confidence intervals, effective detection radius (EDR), and goodness of fit statistics for song detections by species and park. The best model selected through an information-theoretic and goodness of fit model selection process is shown. Model-fitting issues that may affect interpretability are shown in addition to goodness of fit statistics

Common name	Park	Key / adj.[1]	Model[2]	K	Density (birds/ha)	95 % CI	Bootstrap density (birds/ha)	95 % CI	EDR (m)	x^2 GOF p	Cramer-von Mises GOF p	Model issues[3]
Audubon's Warbler	CRLA	HZ C	O	3	1.08	(0.97 - 1.20)	1.20	(0.87 - 1.66)	44.57	0.36		C, I
	LAVO	HZ C	-	2	0.15	(0.13 - 0.17)	0.14	(0.03 - 0.21)	117.46	0.59		C, I
Black-headed Grosbeak	WHIS	HN C	O	2	0.15	(0.13 - 0.17)	0.14	(0.09 - 0.19)	100.77	0.20	0.80	
Brewer's Sparrow	LABE	HZ C	O	2	0.07	(0.05 - 0.08)	0.07	(0.05 - 0.09)	106.10	0.20	0.10	C, I
Black-throated Gray Warbler	WHIS	HN C	-	1	0.53	(0.45 - 0.61)	0.45	(0.27 - 0.61)	69.60	0.52		I
Cassin's Vireo	WHIS	HN C	-	1	0.18	(0.14 - 0.22)	0.18	(0.10 - 0.30)	74.96	0.48		I
Hermit Thrush	CRLA	HN C	O	2	0.38	(0.33 - 0.44)	0.39	(0.25 - 0.53)	70.11	0.76		
Lazuli Bunting	LABE	HZ C	-	2	0.13	(0.11 - 0.16)	0.13	(0.03 - 0.18)	97.42	0.22		
Lincoln's Sparrow	LAVO	HN C	-	1	0.17	(0.14 - 0.22)	0.17	(0.08 - 0.26)	89.45	0.75		
Orange-crowned Warbler	WHIS	HZ C	O	3	0.25	(0.23 - 0.29)	0.24	(0.14 - 0.34)	81.44	0.28		
Oregon Junco	CRLA	HZ C	O	3	0.71	(0.64 - 0.80)	0.79	(0.48 - 1.26)	50.77	0.22		C, I
	LAVO	HN C	-	1	0.36	(0.29 - 0.46)	0.26	(0.04 - 0.45)	63.83	0.69		C, I
	WHIS	HN C	-	1	0.13	(0.10 - 0.18)	0.09	(0.01 - 0.17)	74.87	0.62		C, I
Pacific Wren	RNSP	HN C	O	2	0.48	(0.42 - 0.55)	0.39	(0.14 - 0.61)	70.80	0.21		
Pacific-slope Flycatcher	RNSP	HZ C	-	2	0.69	(0.46 - 1.02)	0.69	(0.48 - 0.90)	52.52	0.00	0.70	
Spotted Towhee	LABE	HZ C	-	2	0.45	(0.41 - 0.50)	0.50	(0.17 - 0.88)	85.53	0.55		
	WHIS	HN C	O	2	0.20	(0.18 - 0.23)	0.17	(0.09 - 0.25)	84.10	0.00	0.50	C, I

[1] Key / adjustment functions of models are abbreviated as: HN C = half-normal cosine, HZ C = hazard cosine.

[2] Model scale parameter covariates and stratification terms, abbreviated as: F = frame, S = song / non-song detection, C = call / not-call detection, O = observer. F * O indicates, for example, that the best model was stratified by frame and contained an effect of observer on the scale parameter that varied by frame. A '-' indicates no covariates were included in the best model.

[3] Model issues are abbreviated as follows: C = model constrained to have no adjustment parameters, B = bootstrap density estimates did not converge on maximum likelihood values, I = data pooled into intervals because of evidence of avoidance or heaping.

10

Table 2 (continued). Detectability models, density estimates, confidence intervals, effective detection radius (EDR), and goodness of fit statistics for song detections by species and park. The best model selected through an information-theoretic and goodness of fit model selection process is shown. Model-fitting issues that may affect interpretability are shown in addition to goodness of fit statistics.

Common name	Park	Key / adj.[1]	Model[2]	K	Density (birds/ha)	95 % CI	Bootstrap density (birds/ha)	95 % CI	EDR (m)	x^2 GOF p	Cramer-von Mises GOF p	Model issues[3]
Swainson's Thrush	RNSP	HN C	-	1	0.05	(0.03 - 0.07)	0.03	(0.01 - 0.06)	151.94	0.53	0.80	
Varied Thrush	RNSP	HN C	O	2	0.13	(0.11 - 0.16)		104.32	0.67		B, I	
Warbling Vireo	LAVO	HN C	-	1	0.13	(0.11 - 0.17)	0.11	(0.04 - 0.18)	92.62	0.61		-
Western Meadowlark	LABE	HN C	O	2	0.24	(0.22 - 0.25)	0.20	(0.12 - 0.27)	152.49	0.09		-
Western Tanager	CRLA	HN C	F	4	0.33	(0.26 - 0.40)	0.32	(0.21 - 0.44)	53.23	0.27	0.50	
	LAVO				0.03	(0.02 - 0.04)	0.03	(0.02 - 0.04)	185.00	0.02	0.30	
	WHIS				0.06	(0.05 - 0.08)	0.05	(0.02 - 0.08)	114.86	0.12	0.60	
Wilson's Warbler	LAVO	HZ	O	4	0.20	(0.18 - 0.22)		73.44	0.06		C, B, I	
	RNSP				0.36	(0.33 - 0.39)		73.44	0.06			

[1] Key / adjustment functions of models are abbreviated as: HN C = half-normal cosine, HZ C = hazard cosine.

[2] Model scale parameter covariates and stratification terms, abbreviated as: F = frame, S = song / non-song detection, C = call / not-call detection, O = observer. F * O indicates, for example, that the best model was stratified by frame and contained an effect of observer on the scale parameter that varied by frame. A '-' indicates no covariates were included in the best model.

[3] Model issues are abbreviated as follows: C = model constrained to have no adjustment parameters, B = bootstrap density estimates did not converge on maximum likelihood values, I = data pooled into intervals because of evidence of avoidance or heaping.

11

Analysis suggested that there may be significant problems with meeting the assumptions of distance sampling for all species that are of potential monitoring interest. Examples of observer avoidance or attraction suggested failure to meet two assumptions, first that all birds are detected at the point and second, that birds are detected prior to any movement in response to the observer (Figures 1A, 1B). An example of heaping suggested that the assumption that distances are always measured accurately may also be a concern (Figure 1C). The distribution of detection distances in some species showed strong evidence of either avoidance behavior or heaping by observers, resulting in a need to combine data into intervals for analysis (Table 1). This problem was especially apparent in the distribution of song detections (Table 2). Further, some models showed lack of fit despite combining data into intervals, and some models failed to converge on maximum likelihood parameter estimates during bootstrap sub-sampling, suggesting sensitivity to the exclusion of a portion of the sample (Tables 1, 2). Some of the 'best' models for each species or park reported did show lack of fit and likely violation of assumptions, and thus their results must be interpreted with caution.

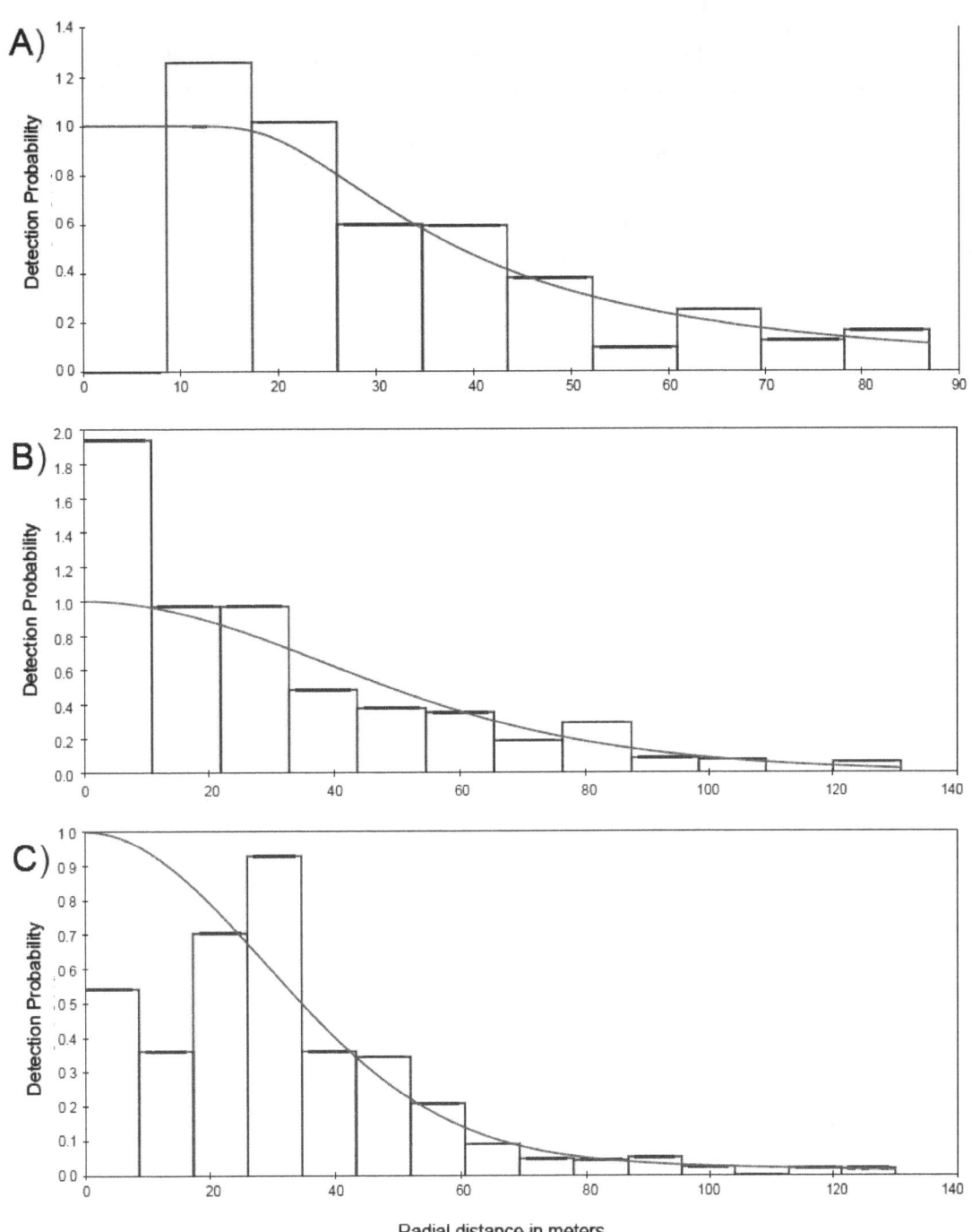

Figure 1. Observed (bars) and expected (curves) distributions of observations by distance. The expected distributions are based upon the assumptions made by Program Distance that detection probability declines monotonically with distance, that individuals do not move in response to observers, and that all distances are measured accurately. The three species shown apparently did not meet one or more of these assumptions. A) Pacific-slope Flycatchers at Redwood National and State Parks showed evidence of observer avoidance, and no birds were detected at the point. B) Brown-headed Cowbirds at Lava Beds National Monument showed evidence of observer attraction, and birds were more likely to be detected at the point. C) Gray Jays at Crater Lake National Park showed evidence of heaping, and birds were most likely to be detected around 30 m.

Density estimates of all detections were highly correlated with density estimates of song detections for a diverse sample of species (Figure 2). However, many of the models of all detections included effects of detection type (Table 1), suggesting that there is a difference in detectability of alternative detection types (e.g. visual, song). Further, the proportion of the total sample that consisted of songs was negatively correlated with the difference between density from total detections and density from song detections (Figure 3). Yet, despite some potential biases associated with estimating densities using the alternative approaches suggested by these results (Figure 3), density estimates from these two approaches are highly correlated (Figure 2).

Analytical density estimates by park and species derived from models using all detections and estimates derived from song detections were highly correlated ($N = 25$, $r = 0.76$, $p < 0.001$; Figure 2), as were bootstrap estimates ($N = 18$, $r = 0.62$, $p < 0.001$). The proportion of the total number of detections that were song detections was negatively correlated with the difference between density estimates from models of all detections and density estimates from models of song detections ($N = 25$, $r = -0.53$, $p = 0.006$; Figure 3).

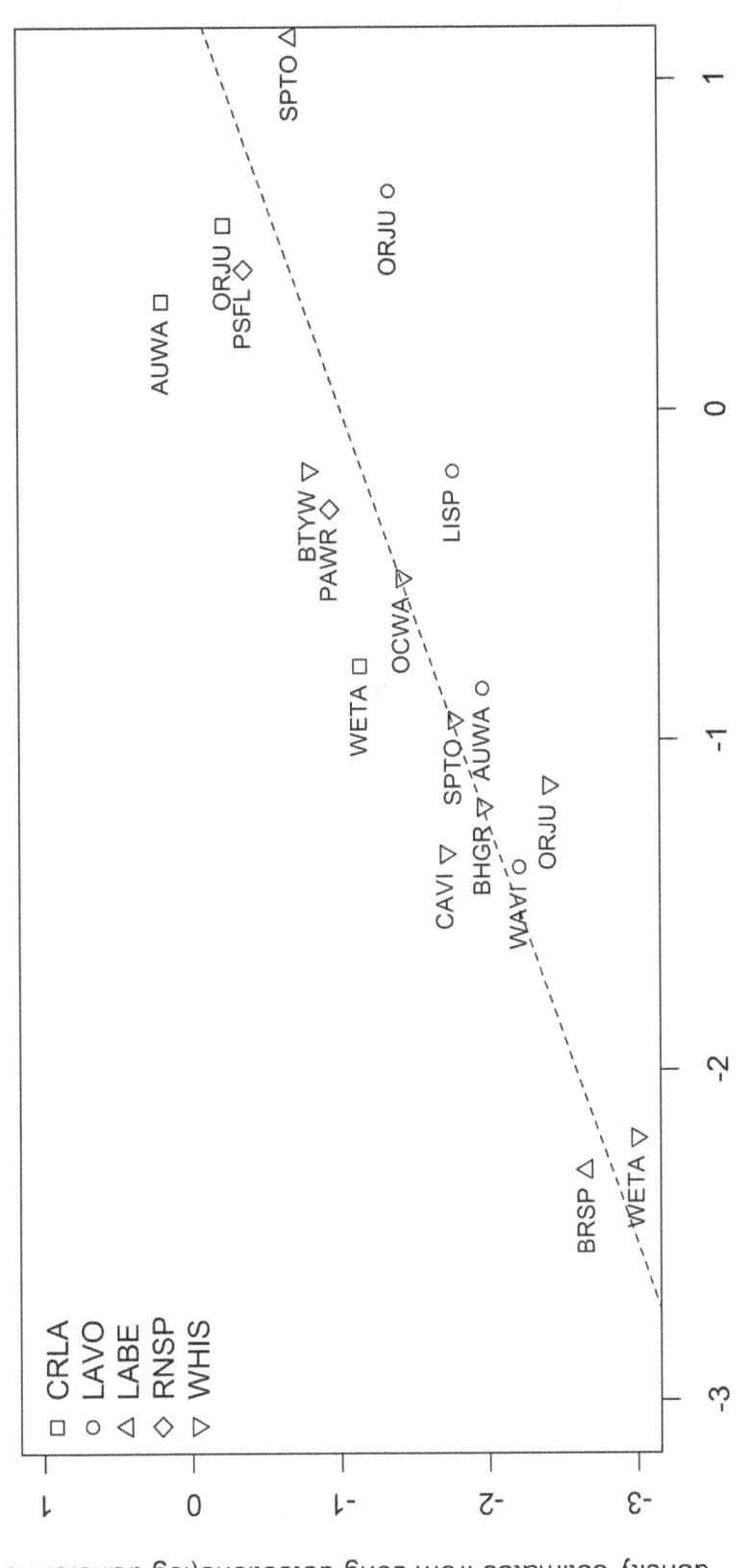

Figure 2. Relationship between log density estimates from models of all detections and log density estimates from song detections (multiplied by 2 to account for non-singing females). The line shown is the 1:1 line. Log density estimates from the two approaches were highly correlated (N = 25, r = 0.76, p < 0.001).

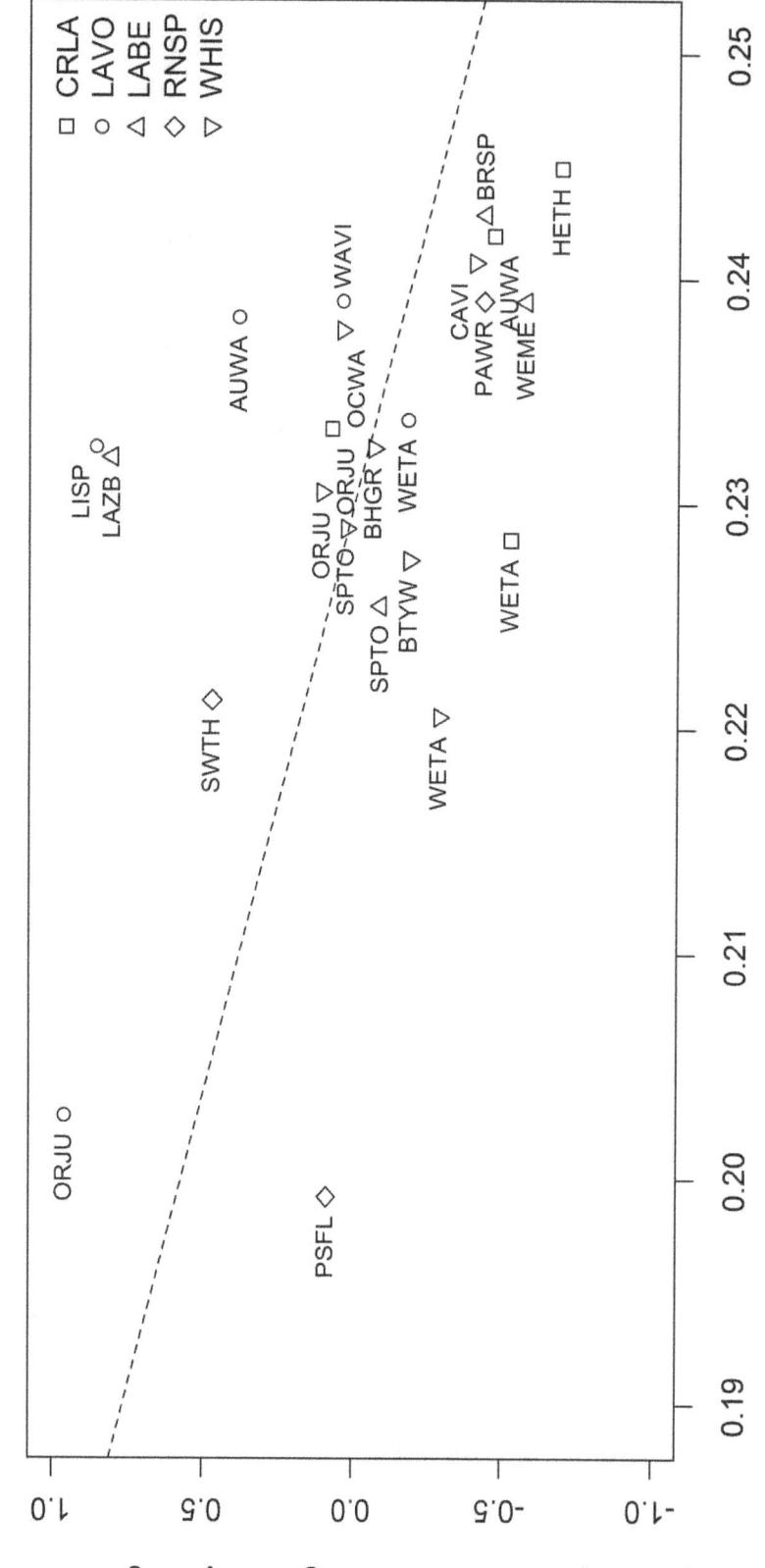

Figure 3. Proportion of song detections in each sample (Freeman-Tukey double-arcsine transformed) and the difference between log density of total detections and log density of song detections are negatively correlated (N = 25, r = -0.53, p = 0.006; Figure 2). The difference between density estimated from total detections and density estimated from song detections thus increased with greater proportions of song detections.

16

Discussion

Estimating detectability is important in monitoring population trends, enumerating habitat associations, and examining bird community structure. Wide variation among species and among parks within species in effective detection radius (EDR) suggests that assuming true density to be proportional to counts among sites and species may be untenable. Results suggesting EDR varies among species are not surprising given that vocalizations differ in volume and resonance. Observer ability may also be an important consideration in study design (Diefenbach et al. 2003). Our results suggest that differences among observers in their ability to hear and identify species by song and sight had strong effects on estimates of detectability, which has implications for both future analysis and protocol implementation. Specifically, limiting surveys within a park in a given year to two observers will increase the sample size of observer/species records, thus increasing the number of species that can be analyzed for detectability in which observer bias is adequately accounted for. Because each park has only been surveyed once, it is difficult to know at this time whether observer bias is confounded with differences in detectability by park. We took a conservative approach in this analysis by separating parks, but grouping parks in future analyses could be considered to bolster sample size. Poor model fit related to issues such as observer avoidance or heaping reiterate that model-based analysis methods for diverse species assemblages may not always appropriately estimate parameters of interest, suggesting that indices such as relative abundance may still be useful in some contexts (Johnson 2008). However, given the evidence for variation among species and parks in EDR and detectability, it is important to consider density estimation when plausible, or use such EDR results to inform how indices of relative abundance are calculated.

These results suggest that while densities estimated from all detections or song detections are similar, species with a very large (> 80%) proportion of song detections may have their densities underestimated by inclusion of all detections. Alternatively, this correlation may be viewed as evidence that inclusion of all detections in species with a lower proportion of song detections causes overestimation of density. These alternatives are impossible to separate without an independently derived measure of density from a technique such as spot-mapping or mark-recapture (e.g. DeSante 1986). These results suggest the importance of considering alternative approaches for estimating density that reflect species biology and species-specific distributions of detection distance and type.

 These analyses provide methodological considerations that will be useful in future efforts to monitor birds within the KLMN. Detectability and its effects on estimated density or relative abundance may be an important consideration in monitoring bird population trends, determining habitat associations, and examining bird community structure. However, species that are somewhat abundant, yet lack sufficient detections for density estimation, may still be sufficiently monitored by relative abundance indices and this consideration is important in planning future analyses. Thus, consideration of species-specific aspects of detectability and abundance should be made when analyzing and interpreting results from broad-scale multiple species monitoring projects such as the KLMN (Stephens et al. *In Review*).

Literature Cited

Altman, B. 1999. Conservation strategy for landbirds in coniferous forests of western Oregon and Washington. Version 1.0. Oregon-Washington Partners in Flight. Online. (http://www.orwapif.org/pdf/western_forest.pdf). Accessed 26 February 2011.

Altman, B. 2000. Conservation strategy for landbirds in of the east-slope of the Cascade Mountains in Oregon and Washington. Version 1.0. Oregon-Washington Partners in Flight. Online. (http://www.orwapif.org/pdf/east_slope.pdf). Accessed 26 February 2011.

Buckland, S. T., D. R. Anderson, K. P. Burnham, J. L. Laake, D. L. Borchers, and L. Thomas. 2001. *Introduction to distance sampling - Estimating abundance of biological populations*. Oxford University Press, Oxford.

Buckland, S. T., D. R. Anderson, K. P. Burnham, J. L. Laake, D. L. Borchers, and L. Thomas. 2004. *Advanced Distance Sampling*. Oxford University Press, Oxford.

Burnham, K. P., and D. R. Anderson. 2002. *Model selection and multi-model inference: a practical information-theoretic approach.* Springer-Verlag, New York, NY.

California Partners in Flight (CalPIF). 2002a. The draft coniferous forest bird conservation plan: A strategy for protecting and managing coniferous forest habitats and associated birds in California (J. Robinson and J. Alexander, lead authors). Version 1.0. Point Reyes Bird Observatory, Stinson Beach, CA. Online. (www.prbo.org/calpif/plans.html). Accessed 4 March 2009.

California Partners in Flight (CalPIF). 2002b. The oak woodland bird conservation plan: A strategy for protecting and managing oak woodland habitats and associated birds in California (S. Zack, lead author). Version 2.0. Online. (www.prbo.org/calpif/plans.html). Accessed 4 March 2009.

California Partners in Flight (CalPIF). 2004. The coastal scrub and chaparral bird conservation plan: A strategy for protecting and managing coastal scrub and chaparral habitats and associated birds in California (J. Lovio, lead author). Version 2.0. PRBO Conservation Science, Stinson Beach, CA. Online. (www.prbo.org/calpif/plans.html). Accessed 4 March 2009.

California Partners in Flight (CalPIF). 2005. The sagebrush bird conservation plan: A strategy for protecting and managing sagebrush habitats and associated birds in California. Version 1.0. PRBO Conservation Science, Stinson Beach, CA. Online. (www.prbo.org/calpif/plans.html). Accessed 4 March 2009.

DeSante, D. F. 1986. A field test of the variable circular-plot censusing method in a Sierran subalpine forest. Condor 88:129-142.

Diefenbach, D. R, D. W. Brauning, and J. A. Mattice. 2003. Variability in grassland bird counts related to observer differences and species detection rates. Auk 120:1168-1179.

Emlen, J. T. 1971. Population densities of birds derived from transect counts. Auk 88:323–342.

Fancy, S. G. 1997. A new approach for analyzing bird densities from variable circular-plot counts. Pacific Science 51:107-114.

Fancy, S. G., and J. R. Sauer. 2000. Recommended methods for inventorying and monitoring landbirds in National Parks. U. S. Department of the Interior. Online. (http://science.nature.nps.gov/im/monitor/protocols/npsbird.doc). Accessed 26 February 2011.

Hussell, D. J. T., and C. J. Ralph. 2005. Recommended methods for monitoring bird populations by counting and capture of migrants. North American Bird Bander 30: 6-20.

Johnson, D. H. 2008. In defense of indices: The case of bird surveys. Journal of Wildlife Management 72:857-868.

Marques, T. A., L. Thomas, S. G. Fancy, and S. T. Buckland. 2007. Improving estimates of bird density using multiple-covariate distance sampling. Auk 124:1229-1243.

Mills, L.S. 2012. *Conservation of wildlife populations: Demography, genetics, and management* (2nd Ed.). Wiley-Blackwell Publishers, Oxford.

Nelson, J. T. and S. G. Fancy. 1999. A test of the variable circular-plot method when exact density of a bird population was known. Pacific Conservation Biology 5:139-143.

Norvell, R. E., F. P. Home, and J. R. Parrish. 2003. A seven-year comparison of relative abundance and distance-sampling methods. Auk 120:1013-1028.

Odion, D., D. Sarr, B. Truitt, A. Duff, S. Smith, W. Bunn, E. Beever, S. Shafer, J. Rocchio, S. Smith, R. Hoffman, and others. 2005. Vital signs monitoring plan for the Klamath Network: Phase II report. U.S. Department of the Interior, National Park Service, Klamath Inventory and Monitoring Network, Ashland, OR.

Reynolds, R. T., J. M. Scott, and R. A. Nussbaum. 1980. A variable circular-plot method for estimating bird numbers. Condor 82:309-313.

Rich, T. D., C. J. Beardmore, H. Berlanga, P. J. Blancher, S. W. Bradstreet, G.S. Butcher, D.W. Demarest, E.H. Dunn, W.C. Hunter, E.E. Iñigo-Elis, and others. 2004. Partners in Flight North American landbird conservation plan. Cornell Lab of Ornithology, Ithaca, NY.

Rosenstock, S.S., D.R. Anderson, K.M. Giesen, T. Leukering, and M.F. Carter. 2002. Landbird counting techniques: current practices and an alternative. The Auk 119:46-53.

Sarr, D. A., D. C. Odion, S. R. Mohren, E. E. Perry, R. L. Hoffman, L. K. Bridy, and A. A. Merton. 2007. Klamath Network Vital Signs Monitoring Plan. Natural Resource Report NPS/KLMN/NRR--2007/016. National Park Service, Fort Collins, Colorado.

Sarr, D. A., S. McCullough, and S. R. Mohren. 2011. Partnering to conserve avian biodiversity in National Parks of the Klamath region. *In* J. L. Stephens, K. Kreitinger, C. J. Ralph, and M. T. Green editors. Informing ecosystem management: Science and process for landbird conservation in the western United States. Biological Technical Publication FWS/ BTP-R1014- 2011, edited by. Portland, Oregon: U.S. Department of Agriculture, Fish and Wildlife Service.

Scott, J. M., F. L. Ramsey, and C. B. Kepler. 1981. Distance estimation as a variable in estimating bird numbers from vocalizations. *In* C. J. Ralph and J. M. Scott, editors. Estimating numbers of terrestrial birds. Studies in Avian Biology 6:334-340.

Stephens, J. L., S. R. Mohren, J. D. Alexander, D. A. Sarr, and K. M. Irvine. 2010a. Klamath Network landbird monitoring protocol. U.S. Department of Interior, National Park Service, Natural Resource Report NPS/KLMN/NRR-2010/187.

Stephens, J. L., J. D. Alexander, and S. R. Mohren. 2010b. Establishment of survey sites for monitoring landbirds within the Klamath Network. U.S. Department of Interior, National Park Service, Natural Resource Data Series NPS/KLMN/NRDS-2010/126.

Stephens, J. L., S. R. Mohren, F. L. Newell, J. D. Alexander, and D. A. Sarr. *In Review.* Bird-habitat associations at five national park units in southern Oregon and northern California. Natural Resource Technical Report NPS/XXXX/NRTR—20XX/XXX. National Park Service, Fort Collins, Colorado.

Thomas, L., S.T. Buckland, E.A. Rexstad, J. L. Laake, S. Strindberg, S. L. Hedley, J. R.B. Bishop, T. A. Marques, and K. P. Burnham. 2010. Distance software: design and analysis of distance sampling surveys for estimating population size. Journal of Applied Ecology 47: 5-14.

Thompson III, F. R. and F. A. LaSorte. 2008. Comparison of methods for estimating bird abundance and trends from historical count data. Journal of Wildlife Management 72:1674-1682.

The Department of the Interior protects and manages the nation's natural resources and cultural heritage; provides scientific and other information about those resources; and honors its special responsibilities to American Indians, Alaska Natives, and affiliated Island Communities.

February 2013

www.ingramcontent.com/pod-product-compliance
Lightning Source LLC
Chambersburg PA
CBHW080941290526
45795CB00007BA/2848